GramClass Plus Workbook 4

Author Hyunjeong, Kim | **Consultant** Prof. Eunyoung, Park |
Editorial Supervisor LLS English Research Center

JPLUS
Language Publishing Co.

I Want Some Cheese

A Write in the correct numbers and trace.

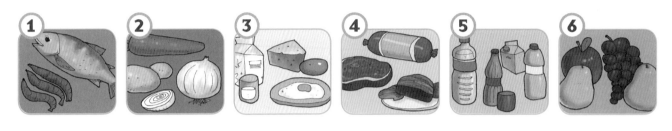

○ vegetables   ○ fruits

○ seafood   ○ dairy products

○ meat   ○ beverages

B Fill in the blanks to complete the cartoons.

Mom, _____ we have _____ bread?

No, we _____.

Then, do we _____ _____ cheese and eggs?

_____. We don't have any _____ and eggs. _____ we have _____ things to buy.

C Complete the sentences with *any* or *some*.

1 I need _____ eggs to make soup.

2 Is there _____ butter in the freezer?

3 I don't have _____ milk to drink.

4 Please cook _____ potatoes for dinner.

5 There isn't _____ cheese in the kitchen.

D Fill in the blanks.

Dad and I are making a _____ _____.
First, we need _____ carrots and potatoes.
_____, we need _____ chicken.
Then, we need _____ mushrooms, too.
We have _____ onions in the refrigerator,
so we don't need _____ more onions.
Let's go _____, Dad.

shopping list
some
any
Second
shopping

E Translate into English.

1. 나는 버터가 약간 필요해.

_____

2. 냉장고에 달걀이 좀 있니?

_____

A Complete the words and write their meanings.

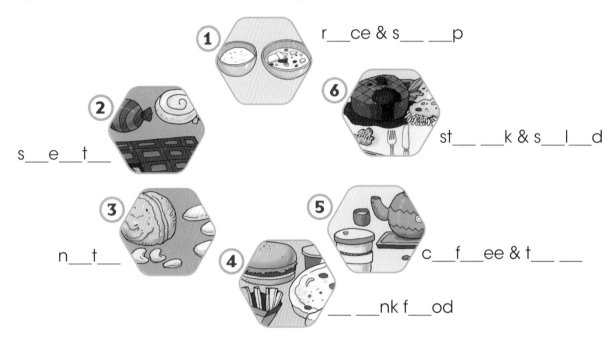

1 r__ce & s___ ___p

2 s__e__t__

6 st__ ___k & s__l__d

3 n__t__

5 c__f__ee & t___ ___

4 __ ___nk f__od

B Fill in the blanks to complete the cartoons.

Do you drink _____water?

Yes. I drink _____ _____ of water.

I drink ten _____ of water ___ _____.

Are you _____?

No. I'm _____.

_____, drinking _____ much water is not good _____ me.

C Complete the sentences using the given expressions.

(1) a lot of

Gram ate _____ rice and soup.

(2) much

Gram doesn't drink _____ coke.

(3) a lot of

There's _____ honey.

(4) a lot of / much

How _____ milk did Greta drink?

She was thirsty. She drank _____ milk.

D Fill in the blanks.

We should eat a _____ of fresh fruits and vegetables _____ day.
_____, we should not eat _____ much _____ food like
hamburgers, pizza, and fried chicken.
Junk food has too _____ calories and too _____ fat.
Junk food has a _____ of salt, _____.
Eat a _____ diet and keep _____.

every
junk
balanced
However
lot
healthy
too
many
much

E Translate into English.

1. 너는 어제 물을 얼마나 마셨니? (How much water)

_____

2. 난 물을 많이 마셨어. (a lot of)

_____

A Complete the words and the expressions and write down each meaning.

(1) e_____

(2) _____ a hand

(3) _____ a problem

(4) sit _____

(5) _____ English

(6) take _____

B Fill in the blanks to complete the cartoons.

Does Jason _____ English _____?

Yes, he _____. He studies _____.

Does he _____ math problems _____?

_____, he does.

How _____ you, Gram?

No, I _____. But I eat _____ fast!

C Complete the sentences using the given hints and the correct adverbs of the given adjectives.

(1) kind

→ The teacher explained _____.

(2) hard / study

→ Gram tries to _____ _____.

(3) good / English

→ Greta speaks _____ _____.

D Change the given adjectives into the correct adverbs and fill in the blanks.

Rules For The Test!

Take your seat (quick) _____ and listen (careful) _____.

Pass out the tests (quick) _____.

When you have a question, please raise your hand (quiet) _____.

Don't talk (loud) _____ with your classmates.

Read and answer the questions (careful) _____.

After the test, leave the classroom (quiet) _____.

E Translate into English.

1. Gram은 그 선생님의 이야기를 주의 깊게 들었다. (carefully / listen to)

_____

2. Greta는 수학 문제들을 빨리 풀었다. (quickly / solve the math problems)

_____

A Write down the correct expressions for the meanings and give the correct letter of the pictures to each expression.

1 잠자리에 들다 → _____ ◯

2 책가방을 싸다 → _____ ◯

3 잠자리에서 일어나다 → _____ ◯

4 숙제를 하다 → _____ ◯

5 샤워를 하다 → _____ ◯

6 아침밥을 먹다 → _____ ◯

B Complete the cartoons.

C Complete the sentences using the given hints.

NEVER 1. watch TV	SELDOM 2. pack a schoolbag	SOMETIMES 3. take a shower
OFTEN 4. make cookies	USUALLY 5. be late for school	ALWAYS 6. play basketball

1 at night → Gram _____.

2 in the morning → Greta _____.

3 before breakfast → Gramson _____.

4 together → Gram and Greta _____.

5 not → Greta _____.

6 after school → Gramson _____.

D Fill in the blanks.

I a_____ get up early. I u_____ take a shower in the morning.
_____ breakfast, I a_____ walk to school.
I am n_____ late _____ school. After school, I a_____ do
my homework first.
Then I o_____ play with my friends or read a book.
I always have dinner _____ my family.
After dinner, I s_____ watch TV.
I a _____ go to bed _____ 10 o'clock.

never
always
sometimes
often
usually
before
after
for
with

E Translate into English.

1. 나는 자주 아침식사로 시리얼을 먹어. (often / cereal)

_____

2. 나는 항상 밤에 숙제를 해. (always / at night)

_____

A Write down the correct expressons.

| gather eggs | unload a truck | shear sheep |
| pick apples | feed a calf | milk a cow |

①

_____

②

_____

③

_____

④

_____

⑤

_____

⑥

_____

B Complete the cartoons.

I'm _____ the cow and _____ eggs. Greta, can you help _____ ?

OK.

I'm _____ sheep and _____ a baby pig. Can you help me, Greta?

OK.

Oh, my! I'm _____ the eggs!

Oh, dear. I'll _____ you.

Please! The sheep is running _____ !

What a _____ !

C **Unscramble the sentences and fill in the blanks using the proper object pronouns for the underlined words.**

(1) a hairband / for <u>his sister</u> / . / bought

→ Gram _____.

→ Gram loves _____.

(2) . / a letter / to <u>John</u> / wrote

→ Greta _____.

→ She likes _____.

(3) <u>an apple pie</u> / . / made

→ Grandma _____.

→ She gave _____ to Greta.

D **Fill in the blanks.**

My grandfather_____ a huge farm.

Today Gramson and I _____ him _____ his farm.

We were _____ a cow. Suddenly a big goose _____ Gramson.

He was so shocked he _____ the egg basket _____ mistake.

All the eggs broke. What a mess! But grandfather just _____ us smiling,

"It's OK, guys. I still _____ you very much."

"We love you too, Grandpa!"

love
hugged
on
kicked
has
helped
surprised
by
milking

E **Translate into English.**

1. Gram은 지금 영어 공부를 하고 있어. (study English / now)

_____

2. 난 어제 영화 한 편을 봤어. (watch a movie / yesterday)

_____

My Friends Sent Me Presents

A Unscramble the words.

1

sneakers
Gramson
lend

_____

2

his photos
sell
the girl

_____

3

Greta
a CD
give

_____

4

show
a model robot
Greta

_____

B Fill in the blanks to complete the cartoons.

My friends _____ me a lot of presents.
Greta, can I _____ you my presents?

A CD and a T-shirt and
sneakers, and a….

KNOCK KNOCK

Knock, knock. Is
_____ there?

Hi, guys. I _____ you the wrong parcels
yesterday. Can you _____ them back?

Oh, my!

Yes, here they
_____.

C Unscramble the senences.

1 the boy's / found / . / toy car / He

→ _____

2 . / some cookies / She / Gram / gave

→ _____

3 passed / the comic books / I / . / Gram

→ _____

D Complete the sentences with the same meaning of the given sentences.

1 Gram bought blue sneakers for Gramson.

→ Gram _____.

2 I lent a bat and a glove to Greta.

→ I _____.

3 He gave a CD and a bag to me.

→ He _____.

E Fill in the blanks.

Many students _____ their teachers some old and new things for the school _____. Greta brought her teacher a pink T-shirt. The teacher _____ us how to sell our things.
And the bazaar opened. Gramson _____ a boy his old model robot.
I _____ the other students Taekwondo _____, too.
It was a great time to share and help _____.

taught
showed
each other
brought
sold
bazaar
performances

F Translate into English.

1. Gram은 Greta에게 그 수학 문제를 물어보았다. (a math problem / ask)

_____

2. 나는 내 남동생에게 책을 한 권 사 주었다. (a book / buy)

_____

Unit 07 Look At That Guy Playing The Guitar

A Connect each picture with its correct expression.

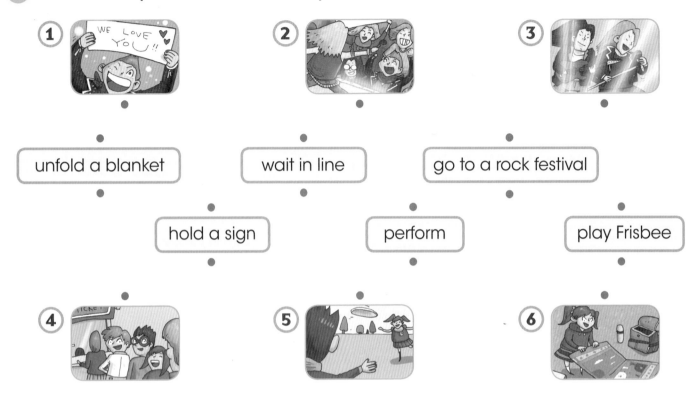

unfold a blanket

wait in line

go to a rock festival

hold a sign

perform

play Frisbee

B Fill in the blanks to complete the cartoons.

C **Unscramble the senences.**

1 go out secretly / Greta / felt

→ Gram _____.

2 watched / win the game / his team

→ Gramson _____.

3 buy some ice cream / Gram / looked at

→ Greta _____.

D **Complete the sentences using the given hints.**

1 play Frisbee / Greta / saw

→ I _____.

2 play the drums / Gram / heard

→ I _____.

E **Fill in the blanks.**

I went to a rock _____ with Greta and Gramson.
We saw many people _____ before the festival. We watched
a popular band _____. We could hear many people _____.
It was so cool! Gramson looked at a girl _____ a sign in _____
of the stage. I _____ Gramson falling in love with her. When the girl
turned _____, we saw that she was a young boy!

shouting
wait in line
around
perform
front
felt
holding
festival

F **Translate into English.**

1. 나는 내 여동생이 노래를 부르고 있는 것을 들었다. (hear / singing)

_____

2. Greta는 Gram이 창문을 깨는 것을 지켜보았다. (watch / break the window)

_____

Please Make Greta Set The Table

A Fill in the blanks and write down the meanings.

1 _____ the food

→ _____

2 _____ the _____

→ _____

3 _____ the room

→ _____

4 ____ ____ the trash

→ _____

5 _____ one's hair _____

→ _____

6 ____ ____ the candles

→ _____

B Fill in the blanks to complete the cartoons.

C Unscramble the senences.

1 serve the food / Greta / for dinnner / made

→ Gram _____.

2 Gram / had / feed his dog

→ Gramson _____.

3 let / Gram / blow out the candles

→ Greta _____.

D Make sentences using the given hints.

1 made / clean up the trash / Greta

→ I _____.

2 had / finish his homework / Gram

→ Gram's mom _____.

E Fill in the blanks.

I had my birthday party yesterday.

Greta and Gramson helped me _____ the party.

I let them _____ the to-do list. I made Gramson _____ the room.

I had Greta _____ the table and food.

Suddenly it started to rain _____. So, none of my friends could come.

So we ate all the snacks and sweets.

Then, today all three of us had our teeth _____ at the dental clinic

_____ all those sweets...

filled
decorate
prepare
because of
heavily
know
set

F Translate into English.

1. Gram은 Greta가 그의 스마트폰을 사용하도록 허락해 주었다. (let / use his smart phone)

_____

2. Greta는 Gram을 방과 후에 기다리게 만들었다. (make / wait after school)

_____

A Complete the words and write their meanings.

1. _____ the guitar
   _____

2. _____ a _____
   _____

3. make _____
   _____

4. watch _____
   _____

5. make a _____ _____
   _____

6. _____ with
   _____

B Fill in the blanks to complete the cartoons.

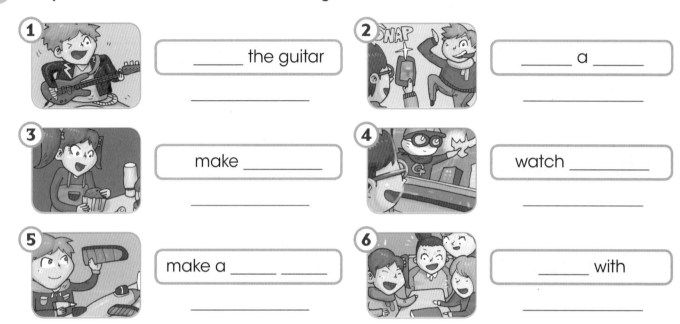

I like _____ to school. My friends are really _____.

Oh, you _____? I _____ going to school.

They are always _____. They love _____ and studying.

I know I _____ _____ study hard _____ them.

_____ we can _____ doing other things.

Right. I enjoy _____ cartoons.

I like _____ _____ airplanes.

C Complete the sentences to find out what each person likes, enjoys, and hates doing.

(1) play the piano
sing loudly

Greta enjoys _____.
Gram likes _____.

(2) eat chicken
learn French

Gram loves _____.
Greta enjoys _____.

(3) take a shower
try on a mini skirt

Gram hates _____.
Greta hates _____.

(4) study math
go to the dentist's

Greta hates _____.
Gram hates _____.

D Fill in the blanks.

My sister Greta likes _____ dresses.
But she hates _____ her dresses.
My cousin Gramson loves _____ poems.
But he hates _____ his poems.
I enjoy writing _____ _____ others.
But I hate _____ my stories _____ others.
_____ has his or her _____ likes and hates.

own
making
to
writing
reading
Everybody
trying on
for
stories
reciting

E Translate into English.

1. 난 사진 찍는 것을 좋아해. (like)

_____

2. 난 내 친구들과 수다 떠는 것을 즐겨. (enjoy)

_____

A Fill in the blanks and write the meanings.

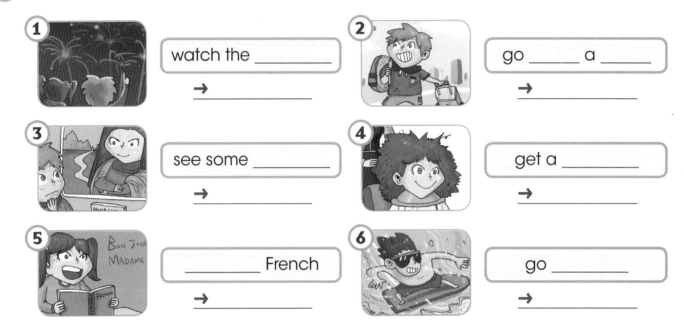

1. watch the _____
   → _____

2. go _____ a _____
   → _____

3. see some _____
   → _____

4. get a _____
   → _____

5. _____ French
   → _____

6. go _____
   → _____

B Fill in the blanks to complete the cartoons.

Greta, where did you decide _____ go this summer?

I _____ to go _____ Paris!

Great! Where do you want to _____ first?

I _____ to visit the Eiffel tower in Paris first.

Can you speak _____ ?

No. So I want _____ _____ French.

Then what do you _____ _____ to do there?

I want to _____ my hair. How _____ this style?

C Write what Gram wants, forgets, and needs to do using the given hints.

FORGET
feed his cat

1 Gram _____.

NEED
study history more

2 Gram _____.

WANT
go scuba diving

3 Gram _____.

D Fill in the blanks by writing the correct forms of the given verbs.

1 Greta expected _____ a new dress. buy

2 Gram is planning _____ some cookies for Greta's birthday. bake

3 Gram hopes _____ a cute girlfriend. meet

E Fill in the blanks.

We want _____ to the mountain. We hope _____.
We also expect _____ under the stars.
Isn't this cool? Greta decided _____ her tent.
Gramson is planning _____ a campfire.
Our summer vacation _____ just perfect!
But, I almost forgot _____ one thing; before the summer
starts, we must get good grades on our exams!

to check
to go
seems
to sleep
to build
to go rafting
to bring

F Translate into English.

1. Greta는 이번 여름에 New York에 방문하고 싶어해. (hope / visit New York)

_____

2. Gram은 등산을 가고 싶어해. (want / go hiking)

_____

A Fill in the blanks and write the correct letters that matches the meanings.

①  ◯

win a _____

②  ◯

_____ rice _____

③  ◯

_____ food

④  ◯

do the _____

⑤  ◯

_____ the contest

⑥  ◯

_____ in _____

a. 무지개 떡   b. 그룹으로 활동하다   c. 발표를 하다
d. 음식을 시식하다   e. 대회에서 우승하다   f. 대회에 참가하다

B Fill in the blanks to complete the cartoons.

Guys! Did you hear _____ the school cooking _____?

No. _____ and _____?

One month _____ now in the school hall.

I want to _____ the contest. Can we work _____ groups?

Cool! So _____ can we make?

_____ _____ a rainbow rice cake?

Great! _____ will find the recipe?

You can, Gram.

C Write the correct question words and answer the questions using the given hints.

(1) Q: _____ bedroom is this?   A: This is Gram's.

(2) Q: _____ does Greta make the rice cake?

A: She learned how to make from her mom.

squash
How
What
Whose
Which

(3) Q: _____ snacks does Gram like?

A: He likes potato chips.

(4) Q: _____ is Gramson's favorite food?

A: His favorite food is pizza.

D Fill in the blanks.

Cooking Contest Registration

1) _____ is your dish? : Rainbow rice cake
2) _____ did you find your recipe? : _____ the internet.
3) _____ did you _____ this dish?
   : I wanted to show everyone a _____ Korean _____.
4) _____ can you make your dish?
   : Please _____ the second file.
5) Which ingredients did you use?
   : Rice _____, autumn squash, etc.

Where
What
How
Why
check
choose
dessert
flour
On
healthy

E Translate into English.

1. 누가 너의 가장 친한 친구니? (best friend)

_____

2. 너는 어느 것을 제일 좋아하니? (best)

_____

A Fill in the blanks.

_____ the _____

_____ bad _____

get _____ _____

get _____

_____ her room

_____ bad eye _____

B Fill in the blanks to complete the cartoons.

Gram, if you eat _____ much, you _____ feel very ill.

Gram, if you don't _____ your room, you _____ find your books.

_____ are my books?

Oh, I'm running _____ of _____!

Gram, if you don't _____ your homework _____ this, you will get bad grades.

_____ you don't _____ up,

we _____ _____ the movie!

C Match the phrases, then write the six sentences.

If-Phrase	Will-Phrase
1. miss the bus	A. get pocket money
2. don't study hard	B. win the cooking contest
3. mow the lawn	C. get ill
4. eat too much	D. be late for the party
5. practice cooking hard	E. get bad grades

(1) If you miss the bus, _____

(2) _____

(3) _____

(4) _____

(5) _____

D Fill in the blanks.

To buy my new bike, I'm _____ to make some pocket money for
it. If I _____ the lawn on Mondays, and if I _____ the dishes
on Tuesdays, and if I _____ my cousin Gramson's model robot
on Wednesdays, and if I do the _____ on Thursdays, and if I take
_____ the trash on Fridays, and if I wash my dad's _____ on
Saturdays, and if I _____ the plants on Sundays, then I _____
get 6,000 won _____ week!
Isn't this great? This is a _____ plan!

water
fix
mow
planning
wash
laundry
car
out
perfect
per
will

E Translate into English.

1. 일요일에 잔디를 깎는다면 난 용돈을 받을 수 있을 거야. (on Sunday)

_____

2. 내 방을 정돈하지 않는다면, 엄마가 화내실 거야. (be angry)

_____

I Am As tall As Steve

A Unscramble the words.

1. u p p l a o r _____

2. h y s _____

3. o t r s n g _____

4. n d i y f e r l _____

5. m r t a s _____

6. k v a t e t l a i _____

B Fill in the blanks to complete the cartoons.

Look _____ me.
I am _____ tall
_____ Steve.

_____ you
as _____ as
Steve?

Yes, I am _____
strong _____ Steve.

Are you as
_____ as Steve?

Of _____. I am _____
smart _____ Steve.

But... _____ I am
_____ _____ smart
_____ Steve.

C Rewrite the sentences using the given hints and (not) as...as.

| We're the same age. | = | I am as old as you (are). |

(1) We are both equally smart. smart = _____.

(2) We are the same height. high = _____.

(3) Greta's writing is good but Gram's is bad. good = _____.

(4) Gram is talkative but I am quiet. talkative = _____.

D Complete the answers using (not) as...as.

(1) Q: Is Gram popular like Steve?   A: No. He _____ Steve.

(2) Q: Does Gram speak French well?   A: Yes. He _____ Greta.

E Fill in the blanks.

I'm Gram and my cousin is Gramson. We look a lot _____.

I'm 12 and he is 15.

I'm 5 feet tall but I'm not as tall as _____. He's 6 feet tall.

Also I'm very _____, so Gramson is not as talkative _____

me. He is quiet.

But we have one thing _____ common. We _____ like cartoons.

I like cartoons as _____ as Gramson _____.

That's _____ we can be _____ friends.

talkative
different
best
both
him
much
as
why
in
does

F Translate into English.

1. Gram은 Steve 만큼 공부를 열심히 해. (as...as / hard)

_____

2. Gram은 Gramson 만큼 기타를 잘 연주하지 못해. (not as...as / well)

_____

A **Write the words and match each with its opposite.**

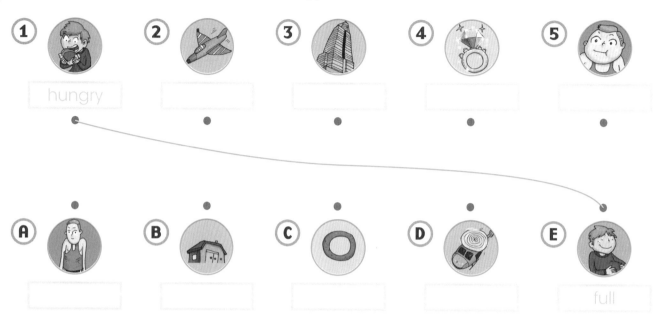

① hungry ② ③ ④ ⑤

A B C D E full

B **Fill in the blanks to complete the cartoons.**

_____ one is faster?

It's _____ your left _____.

_____! Give _____ two.

OK. _____ you are.

Are you _____? Which _____ is higher?

Hmm… In _____ right hand.

Yes, I'm right. I got a _____. Give _____ all your cards!

Oh, my!

C Complete the table.

Adjectives	Comparatives	Adjectives	Comparatives
1. easy		2. fat	
3. hungry		4. expensive	
5. young		6. full	
7. big		8. pretty	
9. good		10. much	
11. bad		12. popular	

D Finish the sentences using the proper comparatives.

1 My writing is bad but his writing is good.   better

→ His writing _____.

2 Gram is 12 years old and Greta is 9 years old.   older

→ Gram _____.

E Fill in the blanks.

This _____ my family will go to Gyeongju.
My dad's car is more _____ _____ a bus.
However, we will _____ an express bus.
It is _____ than driving.
There will be _____ cars on the road this weekend.
However, the bus uses the bus _____ and it _____ only four
hours. Taking a bus is also _____ than driving.
I _____ wait for our trip.

cheaper
weekend
comfortable
faster
can't
takes
lane
more
take
than

E Translate into English.

1. Greta가 Gram보다 더 똑똑해. (smart)

_____

2. Gram의 모자가 Gramson의 것보다 싸. (cheap / cap)

_____

What Is The Tallest Tower?

A Write the words and match each with its opposite.

B Fill in the blanks to complete the cartoons.

Which one of these
is _____ _____
building?

The _____ is
the oldest!

Right! Which one of _____
is ____ _____ tower?

The ____ _____
is the tallest!

Right! This is the _____
one. Who is ____ _____
famous singer?

Gram!
Gram!

I am ____ _____
_____ singer!

C **Complete the table.**

Adjectives	Superlatives	Adjectives	Superlatives
1. narrow		2. wide	
3. heavy		4. famous	
5. short		6. cold	
7. big		8. busy	
9. good		10. much	
11. bad		12. important	

D **Complete or make sentences using an adjective from Box A and a phrase from Box B. Change the adjectives to superlatives.**

A	B
narrow	at that time
famous	in my town
hot	at his school
heavy	in Japan
long	in the spa
fast	in the world

(1) The cheetah is _____ animal _____.

(2) This dinosaur had _____ neck _____.

(3) This pool is _____ one _____.

(4) This road is _____ road _____.

(5) Gramson is _____ student poet _____.

(6) He is _____ sumo wrestler _____.

E **Translate into English.**

1. Greta가 반에서 제일 키가 커. (tall)

_____

2. Gram은 학교에서 가장 웃긴 학생이야. (funny)

_____

A Connect each meaning with its correct picture and write down its English expression.

일기를 쓰다

칠면조를 요리하다

인디언 옥수수로 팝콘을 만들다

_____   _____   _____

감자껍질을 깎다

젓가락으로 음식을 먹다

호박파이를 굽다

_____   _____   _____

B Fill in the blanks to complete the cartoons.

_____ you _____ baked a pumpkin pie?

Uh… no.

Gramson, have you ever _____ Indian popcorn?

Well…no.

Gram, _____ you _____ _____ a turkey?

No.

Then _____ have you _____ _____ for Thanksgiving Day?

We've _____ a lot of turkey.

C Complete the table.

Base Verb	Past Simple	Past Particle	Base Verb	Past Simple	Past Particle
1. is / are			2. give		
3. go			4. forgive		
5. have			6. know		
7. eat			8. come		
9. cook			10. run		

D Write the things Gram has never done and Gram has done once, or a lot of times.

Ever Done Before
1. pop Indian popcorn twice
3. see a snake
5. meet a film star

Never Done
2. peel potatoes
4. eat with chopsticks
6. go fishing

1 Gram has popped Indian popcorn twice.

2 Gram _____.

3 Gram _____.

4 Gram _____.

5 Gram _____.

6 Gram _____.

E Fill in the blanks.

Have you _____ _____ about what you've never done?

Gram's never _____ a pie. He's never _____ a diary.

Gramson has _____ eaten with chopsticks.

And what _____ me? I've never _____ late for school.

I've never _____ my brother's birthday. I've never talked _____ my brothers' back.

never
ever
been
thought
forgotten
baked
kept
about
behind

F Translate into English.

1. 너는 New York에 가 본 적이 있니? (ever / to New York)

_____

2. 난 칠면조를 요리해 본 적이 전혀 없어. (never / cook a turkey)

_____

nswers

Unit 01. p.2

A.

2. vegetables   6. fruits
1. seafood   3. dairy products
4. meat   5. beverages

B.

1. Mom, **do** we have **any** bread?
2. No, we **don't**.
3. Then, do we **have any** cheese and eggs?
4. **Sorry**. We don't have any **cheese** and eggs. **But** we have **many** things to buy.

C.

1. I need **some** eggs to make soup.
2. Is there **any** butter in the freezer?
3. I don't have **any** milk to drink.
4. Please cook **some** potatoes for dinner.
5. There isn't **any** cheese in the kitchen.

D.

Dad and I are making a **shopping list**.
First, we need **some** carrots and potatoes.
Second, we need **some** chicken.
Then, we need **some** mushrooms, too.
We have **some** onions in the refrigerator, so we don't need **any** more onions.
Let's go **shopping**, Dad.

E.

1. **I need some butter.**
2. **Is there any eggs in the freezer?**

Unit 02. p.4

A.

1. r<u>i</u>ce & s<u>ou</u>p   2. sw<u>ee</u>t<u>s</u>
3. n<u>u</u>t<u>s</u>   4. j<u>u</u>nk f<u>oo</u>d
5. c<u>o</u>ff<u>e</u>e & t<u>ea</u>   6. st<u>ea</u>k & s<u>a</u>l<u>a</u>d

B.

1. Do you drink **much** water?
   Yes. I drink **a lot** of water.
2. I drink ten **bottles** of water **a day**.
3. Are you **okay**?
   No, I'm **not**.
4. **Sometimes**, drinking **too** much water is not good **for** me.

C.

1. Gram ate **a lot of** rice and soup.
2. Gram **doesn't** drink **much** coke.
3. There's **a lot of** honey.
4. How **much** milk did Greta drink?
   She was thirsty. She drank **a lot of** milk.

D.

We should eat a **lot** of fresh fruits and vegetables **every** day.
However, we should not eat **too** much **junk** food like hamburgers, pizza, and fried chicken.
Junk food has too **many** calories and too **much** fat.
Junk food has a **lot** of salt, **too**.
Eat a **balanced** diet and keep **healthy**.

E.

1. **How much water did you drink yesterday?**
2. **I drank a lot of water.**

Unit 03. p.6

A.

1. **e**xplain: 설명하다
2. **raise** a hand: 손을 들다
3. **solve** a problem: 문제를 풀다
4. sit **down**: 자리에 앉다
5. **speak** English: 영어를 말하다
6. take **notes**: 필기하다, 기록하다

B.

1. Does Jason **speak** English **well**?
   Yes, he **does**.
   He studies **hard**.
2. Does he **solve** math problems **well**?
   Yes, he does.
3. How **about** you, Gram?
   No, I **don't**. But I eat **really** fast!

C.

1. The teacher explained **kindly**.
2. Gram tries to **study hard**.
3. Greta speaks **English well**.

D.

Rules For The Test!
Take your seat **quickly** and listen **carefully**.
Pass out the tests **quickly**.
When you have a question, please raise your hand **quietly**.
Don't talk **loudly** with your classmates.
Read and answer the questions **carefully**.
After the test, leave the classroom **quietly**.

E.

1. **Gram listened to the teacher carefully.**
2. **Greta solved the math problems quickly.**

Unit 04. p.8

A.

1. 잠자리에 들다: **go to bed** (c)
2. 책가방을 싸다: **pack a schoolbag** (f)
3. (잠자리에서) 일어나다: **get up** (d)
4. 숙제를 하다: **do homework** (b)
5. 샤워를 하다: **take a shower** (e)
6. 아침밥을 먹다: **have breakfast** (a)

B.

1. I **always** get up at 7.
   Really? I **never** get up at 7.
   It's **too** early for me.
2. I **always** do my homework **after** school.
   How **about** you, Gram?
3. I **always** do my homework in the morning.
   I **sometimes** read books before bedtime.
4. Oh, you **too**?
   I **always** read books **before** bedtime **like** you.

C.

1. Gram **never watches TV at night**.
2. Greta **seldom packs a schoolbag in the morning**.
3. Gramson **sometimes takes a shower before breakfast**.
4. Gram and Greta **often make cookies together**.
5. Greta **isn't usually late for school**.
6. Gramson **always plays basketball after school**.

D.

I a**lways** get up early.
I u**sually** take a shower in the morning.
After breakfast, I a**lways** walk to school.
I am n**ever** late **for** school.
After school, I a**lways** do my homework first.
Then I o**ften** play with my friends or read a book.
I always have dinner **with** my family.
After dinner, I s**ometimes** watch TV.
I a**lways** go to bed **before** 10 o'clock.

E.

1. **I often eat (have) cereal for breakfast.**
2. **I always do my homework at night.**

Unit 05. p.10

A.

1. **unload a truck**   2. **gather eggs**
3. **shear sheep**   4. **milk a cow**
5. **feed a calf**   6. **pick apples**

B.

1. I'm **milking** the cow and **gathering** eggs. Greta can you help **me**?
   OK.
2. I'm **shearing** sheep and **feeding** a baby pig. Can you help me, Greta?
   OK.
3. Oh, my! I'm **dropping** the eggs!
   Oh, dear. I'll **help** you.
4. Please! The sheep is running **away**!
   What a **mess**!

C.

1. **Gram bought a hairband for his sister.**
   He loves **her**.
2. **Greta wrote a letter to John.**
   She likes **him**.
3. **Grandma made an apple pie.**
   She gave **it** to Greta.

D.

My grandfather **has** a huge farm.
Today Gramson and I **helped** him **on** his farm.
We were **milking** a cow.
Suddenly a big goose **surprised** Gramson.
He was so shocked he **kicked** the egg basket **by** mistake. All the eggs broke.
What a mess!
But grandfather just **hugged** us smiling, "It's OK, guys. I still **love** you very much."
"We love you too, Grandpa!"

E.

1. **Gram is studying English now.**
2. **I watched a movie yesterday.**

Unit 06. p.12

A.

1. lend Gramson sneakers
2. sell the girl his photos
3. give Greta a CD
4. show Greta a model robot

B.

1. My friends **sent** me a lot of presents.
   Greta, can I **show** you my presents?
2. A CD and a T-shirt and sneakers, and a…
   Knock, knock. Is **anyone** there?
3. Hi, Greta. I **gave** you the wrong parcels yesterday. Can you **give** them back?
   Yes, here they **are**.
   Oh, my!

C.

1. **He found the boy's toy car.**
2. **She gave Gram some cookies.**
3. **I passed Gram the comic books.**

D.

1. Gram **bought Gramson blue sneakers.**
2. **I lent Greta a bat and a glove.**
3. He **gave me a CD and a bag.**

E.

Many students **brought** their teachers some old and new things for the school **bazaar**.
Greta brought her teacher a pink T-shirt.
The teacher **taught** us how to sell our things.
And the bazaar opened.
Gramson **sold** a boy his old model robot.

nswers

I **showed** the other students
Taekwondo **performances**, too.
It was a great time to share and help
each other.

F.

1. **Gram asked Greta a math problem.**
2. **I bought my brother a book.**

Unit 07. p.14

A.

1. **hold a sign**
2. **go to a rock festival**
3. **perform**
4. **wait in line**
5. **play Frisbee**
6. **unfold a blanket**

B.

1. Can you **hear** the rock singer **singing**?
   Yes. Wow! **Look** **at** that guy **playing**
   the guitar.
   By the **way**, Gram. Where's the
   blanket? I **saw** you **folding** it this
   morning.
2. Oh, sorry. I **forgot** it.
   It's OK. I saw a man **barbecuing** over
   there. Can we have some hotdogs?
3. Great! I love hotdogs!
   Alright! But we have to **wait** in **line**.

C.

1. Gram **felt Greta go out secretly**.
2. Gramson **watched his team win the
   game**.
3. Greta **looked at Gram buy some ice
   cream**.

D.

1. I **saw Greta play Frisbee**.
2. I **heard Gram play the drums**.

E.

I went to a rock **festival** with Greta and
Gramson. We saw many people **wait in
line** before the festival.
We watched a popular band **perform**.
We could hear many people **shouting**.
It was so cool!
Gramson looked at a girl **holding** a sign
in **front** of the stage. I **felt** Gramson
falling in love with her.
When the girl turned **around**, we saw
that she was a young boy!

F.

1. **I heard my sister singing.**
2. **Greta watched Gram break the
   window.**

Unit 08. p.16

A.

1. **serve** the food ➡ 음식을 대접하다
2. **set** the **table** ➡ 식탁을 차리다
3. **decorate** the room ➡ 방을 장식하다
4. **clean up** the trash ➡ 쓰레기를 치우다
5. **have** one's **hair cut** ➡ 이발하다
6. **blow out** the candles
   ➡ 촛불을 입으로 불어서 끄다

B.

1. Greta, please have Gramson
   decorate the party room.
   OK.
2. Gramson, please make Greta **serve**
   the food now.
   OK.
3. Greta, can you have the movie **run** now?
   Gramson, can you get the cake **set**
   on the table?
   Now? OK.
4. Now I'm going to have my hair **cut**.

C.

1. Gram **made Greta serve the food**.
2. Gramson **had Gram feed his dog**.
3. Greta **let Gram blow out the candles**.

D.

1. I **made Greta clean up the trash**.
2. Gram's mom **had Gram finish his
   homework**.

E.

I had my birthday party yesterday.
Greta and Gramson helped me **prepare**
the party.
I let them **know** the to-do list.
I made Gramson **decorate** the room.
I had Greta **set** the table and food.
Suddenly it started to rain **heavily**.
So, none of my friends could come.
So we ate all the snacks and sweets.
Then, today all three of us had our teeth
filled at the dental clinic **because of** all
those sweets...

F.

1. **Gram let Greta use his smart phone.**
2. **Greta made Gram wait after school.**

Unit 09. p.18

A.

1. **play** the guitar: 기타를 연주하다
2. **take** a **picture**: 사진을 찍다
3. make **cupcakes**: 컵케이크를 만들다
4. watch **cartoons**: 만화영화를 보다
5. make a **model airplane**: 모형비행기를
   만들다
6. **chat** with: ~와 수다떨다

B.

1. I like **going** to school. My friends are
   really **fun**.
   Oh, you **do**? I **hate** going to school.
2. They are always **busy**. They love

reading and studying.

3. I know I **have** **to** study hard **like** them.
   But we can **enjoy** doing other things.
4. Right. I enjoy **watching** cartoons.
   I like **making** **model** airplanes.

C.

1. Greta enjoys **playing the piano**.
   Gram likes **singing loudly**.
2. Gram loves **eating chicken**.
   Greta enjoys **learning French**.
3. Gram hates **taking a shower**.
   Greta hates **trying on a mini skirt**.
4. Greta hates **studying math**.
   Gram hates **going to the dentist's**.

D.

My sister Greta likes **making** dresses.
But she hates **trying on** her dresses.
My cousin Gramson loves **writing** poems.
But he hates **reciting** his poems.
I enjoy writing **stories for** others.
But I hate **reading** my stories **to** others.
Everybody has his or her **own** likes and hates.

E.

1. **I like taking a picture.**
2. **I enjoy chatting with my friends.**

Unit 10 p.20

A.

1. watch the **fireworks**: 불꽃놀이를 구경하다
2. go **on** a **trip**: 여행 가다
3. see some **paintings**: 작품들을 보다
4. get a **haircut**: 머리카락을 자르다
5. **learn** French: 프랑스어를 배우다
6. go **surfing**: 서핑을 하러 가다

B.

1. Greta, where did you decide **to** go

this summer?
   I **decided** to go **to** Paris!
2. Great! Where do you want to **visit** first?
   I **hope** to visit the Eiffel tower in Paris first.
3. Can you speak **French**?
   No. So I want **to learn** French.
4. Then what do you **want** to do there?
   I want to **do** my hair. How **about** this style?

C.

1. Gram **forgets to feed his cat**.
2. Gram **needs to study history more**.
3. Gram **wants to go scuba diving**.

D.

1. Greta expected **to buy** a new dress.
2. Gram is planning **to bake** some cookies for Greta's birthday.
3. Gram hopes **to meet** a cute girlfriend.

E.

We want **to go** to the mountain. We hope **to go rafting**. We also expect **to sleep** under the stars. Isn't this cool? Greta decided **to bring** her tent. Gramson is planning **to build** a campfire. Our summer vacation **seems** just perfect! But, I almost forgot **to check** one thing; before the summer starts, we must get good grades on our exams!

F.

1. **Greta hopes to visit New York.**
2. **Gram wants to go hiking.**

Unit 11 p.22

A.

1. win a **contest**: **e**
2. **rainbow** rice **cake**: **a**
3. **try** food: **d**

4. do the **presentation**: **c**
5. **attend** the contest: **f**
6. **work** in **groups**: **b**

B.

1. Guys! Did you hear **about** the school cooking **contest**?
   No. **When** and **where**?
2. One month **from** now in the school hall.
   I want to **attend** the contest. Can we work in groups?
3. Cool! So **what** can we make?
   How about a rainbow rice cake?
4. Great! **Who** will find the recipe?
   You can, Gram.

C.

1. **Whose** bedroom is this?
2. **How** does Greta make the rice cake?
3. **Which** snacks does Gram like?
4. **What** is Gramson's favorite food?

D.

Cooking Contest Registration
1) **What** is your dish?
   Rainbow rice cake
2) **Where** did you find your recipe?
   On the internet.
3) **Why** did you **choose** this dish?
   I wanted to show everyone a **healthy** Korean **dessert**.
4) **How** can you make your dish?
   Please **check** the second file.
5) Which ingredients did you use?
   Rice **flour**, autumn squash, etc.

E.

1. **Who is your best friend?**
2. **Which do you like best?**

Unit 12 p.24

A.

1. **mow** the **lawn**   2. **get** bad **grades**

Answers

3. get **pocket** **money**
4. get **ill**   5. **tidy** her room
6. **have** bad eye **sight**

B.

1. Gram, if you eat **too** much, you **will** feel very ill.
2. **Where** are my books?
   Gram, if you don't **tidy** your room, you **won't** find your books.
3. Oh, I'm running **out** of **time**!
   Gram, if you don't **finish** your homework **like** this, you will get bad grades.
4. **If** you don't **hurry** up, we **will** **miss** the movie!

C.

1. If you miss the bus, **you will be late for the party.(D)**
2. **If you don't study hard, you will get bad grades.(E)**
3. **If you mow the lawn, you will get pocket money.(A)**
4. **If you eat too much, you will get ill. (C)**
5. **If you practice cooking hard, you will win the cooking contest.(B)**

D.

To buy my new bike, I'm **planning** to make some pocket money for it.
If I **mow** the lawn on Mondays, and if I **wash** the dishes on Tuesdays, and if I **fix** my cousin Gramson's model robot on Wednesdays, and if I do the **laundry** on Thursdays, and if I take **out** the trash on Fridays, and if I wash my dad's **car** on Saturdays, and if I **water** the plants on Sundays, then I **will** get 6,000 won **per** week!
Isn't this great? This is a **perfect** plan!

E.

1. **If I mow the lawn on Sunday, I'll get pocket money**.
2. **If I don't tidy my room, Mom will be angry**.

Unit 13 p.26

A.

1. **popular**   2. **shy**   3. **strong**
4. **friendly**   5. **smart**   6. **talkative**

B.

1. Look **at** me. I am **as** tall **as** Steve.
2. **Are** you as **strong** as Steve?
   Yes, I am **as** strong **as** Steve.
3. Are you as **smart** as Steve?
   Of **course**. I am **as** smart **as** Steve.
   But… **sometimes** I am **not as** smart **as** Steve.

C.

1. **I am as smart as you.**
2. **I am as high as you.**
3. **Gram's writing is not as good as Greta's writing(hers).**
4. **I am not as talkative as Gram.**

D.

1. No. He **is not as popular as** Steve.
2. Yes. He **speaks French as well as** Greta.

E.

I'm Gram and my cousin is Gramson.
We look a lot **different**.
I'm 12 and he is 15.
I'm 5 feet tall but I'm not as tall as **him**.
He's 6 feet tall.
Also I'm very **talkative**, so Gramson is not as talkative **as** me. He is quiet.
But we have one thing **in** common.

We **both** like cartoons.
I like cartoons as **much** as Gramson **does**.
That's **why** we can be **best** friends.

F.

1. Gram studies as hard as Steve.
2. Gram plays the guitar not as well as Gramson.

Unit 14 p.28

A.

1. **hungry** - E: **full**
2. **fast** - D: **slow**
3. **high** - B: **low**
4. **expensive** - C: **cheap**
5. **fat** - A: **thin**

B.

1. **Which** one is faster?
   It's **in** your left **hand**.
2. **Wrong**! Give **me** two.
   OK. **Here** you are.
3. Are you **ready**? Which **one** is higher?
   Hmm… In **your** right hand.
4. Yes, I'm right. I got a **bonus**. Give **up** all your cards!
   Oh, my!

C.

1. **easier**   2. **fatter**   3. **hungrier**
4. **more expensive**   5. **younger**
6. **fuller**   7. **bigger**   8. **prettier**
9. **better**   10. **more**   11. **worse**
12. **more popular**

D.

1. His writing **is better than mine (my writing)**.
2. Gram **is older than Greta**.

E.

This **weekend** my family will go to

Gyeongju.

My dad's car is **more** comfortable **than** a bus.

However, we will **take** an express bus. It is **faster** than driving.

There will be **more** cars on the road this weekend. However, the bus uses the bus **lane** and it **takes** only four hours.

Taking a bus is also **cheaper** than driving.

I **can't** wait for our trip.

F.

1. Greta is smarter than Gram.
2. Gram's cap is cheaper than Gramson's.

Unit 15 p.30

A.

1. **hot** - C: **cold**   2. **wide** - E: **narrow**
3. **old** - A: **new**   4. **tall** - D: **short**
5. **heavy** - B: **light**

B.

1. Which one of these is **the oldest** building?
   The **Pyramid** is the oldest!
2. Right! Which one of **these** is **the tallest** tower?
   The **CN tower** is the tallest!
3. Right! This is the **last** one.
   Who is **the most** famous singer?
   Gram! Gram!
4. I am **the most famous** singer!

C.

1. **narrowest**   2. **widest**
3. **heaviest**   4. **most famous**
5. **shortest**   6. **coldest**
7. **biggest**   8. **busiest**
9. **best**   10. **most**
11. **worst**   12. **most important**

D.

1. The cheetah is **the fastest** animal **in the world**.
2. This dinosaur had **the longest** neck **at that time**.
3. This pool is **the hottest** one **in the spa**.
4. This road is **the narrowest** road **in my town**.
5. Gramson is **the most famous** student poet **at his school**.
6. He is **the heaviest** sumo wrestler **in Japan**.

E.

1. **Greta is the tallest in her class.**
2. **Gram is the funniest student at school.**

Unit 16 p.32

A.

1: 칠면조를 요리하다 – cook a turkey
2: 감자껍질을 깎다 – peel potatoes
3: 젓가락으로 음식을 먹다 – eat with chopsticks
4: 일기를 쓰다 – keep a diary
5: 호박파이를 굽다 - bake a pumpkin pie
6: 인디언 옥수수로 팝콘을 만든다 – pop Indian popcorn

B.

1. **Have** you **ever** baked a pumpkin pie?
   Uh…no.
2. Gramson, have you ever **popped** Indian popcorn?
   Well…no.
3. Gram, **have** you **ever cooked** a turkey?
   No.
4. Then **what** have you **ever done** for Thanksgiving Day?
   We've **eaten** a lot of turkey.

C.

1. is/are - **was/were** - **been**
2. give - **gave** - **given**
3. go - **went** - **gone**
4. forgive - **forgave** - **forgiven**
5. have - **had** - **had**
6. know - **knew** - **known**
7. eat - **ate** - **eaten**
8. come - **came** - **come**
9. cook - **cooked** - **cooked**
10. run - **ran**- **run**

D.

2. Gram **has never peeled potatoes.**
3. Gram **has seen a snake.**
4. Gram **has never eaten with chopsticks.**
5. Gram **has met a film star.**
6. Gram **has never gone fishing.**

E.

Have you **ever thought** about what you've never done?

Gram's never **baked** a pie.

He's never **kept** a diary.

Gramson has n**ever** eaten with chopsticks.

And what **about** me?

I've never **been** late for school.

I've never **forgotten** my brother's birthday.

I've never talked **behind** my brother's back.

F.

1. **Have you ever been to New York?**
2. **I've never cooked a turkey.**

GramGram Plus 4
Workbook

First Printing 2014.8.20

Author Hyunjeong, Kim

Illustration SeokHi, Kim

Consultant Prof. Eunyoung, Park

Editorial Supervisor LLS English Research Center

Publisher Kiseon, Lee

Publishing Company JPLUS

62, World Cup-ro 31-gil, Mapo-gu, Seoul, Korea

Telephone 02-332-8320

Fax 02-332-8321

Homepage www.jplus114.com

Registration Number 10-1680

Registration Date 1998.12.09

ISBN 979-11-5601-020-3